Broke

But Not *Broken*

By Martha Rushing

Empowerment Publishing & Multi-Media

Martha Rushing

Acknowledgments

Several years ago, I knew this book was supposed to be written I allowed fear, doubt and uncertainty to keep me running circles around the idea of finally becoming an author.

This book is God's divine purpose over my life manifesting, he removed the weeds in my life and planted beautiful flowers. The individuals in my life push me to greatness and when I start to doubt they push me harder. One of those beautiful flowers is the man God blessed me with and I am honored to call my husband, Esteban Rushing.

I thank God daily for allowing me to be covered by someone he perfectly designed for me. A husband that knows the value of his wife and covers her in prayer every moment of the day, my heart skips a beat when I hear him in the corner thanking God for me and praying over my life. I could not ask for anything more in a husband, thank you for creating an environment at home where my purpose can be birthed out of me.

I am grateful for our creations William, Nicolas, Antonio, Shawn, Brianna and Xenia, we get to create a foundation together for each of their futures and watch them soar through life as they manifest every treasure God has placed within them. I would not want to share that journey with no one else but you.

To my mother, thank you for always believing in me, and praying for me. During the most tragic time in my life you prayed for me and without you standing in the gap as my gate keeper my outcome might have been different.

Yvonne Skinner, my ace boon coon, my beautiful bossy sister words can't express my love for you, but you already know all this, you made sure I never lost sight of this book becoming a reality. Thank you for helping through this process making sure whenever there was a need it was met.

Apostle Moton my spiritual mother, thank you for being obedient to the word of God. You saw what God intended for my life and regardless if I resisted you pushed until I was in line with God's will, thank you for always being willing to teach the word and give me corrections when needed.

New Beginnings Ministry Church you all rock and thank you for always uplifting me and supporting me through the journey God has me on.

Apostle Evans last year I still had this book on the inside of me, God wanted it out and he used you as a vessel to give me a word. Thank you for being the Man of God you are, last year your Prophetic word relit my fire.

Last but certainly not least, I want to thank each one of you for always supporting me. Attending my women conferences, showing up to hear me speak at events, joining my Butterfly Nation page on Facebook, sending me messages informing me how my testimony has helped you. I love you all unconditionally, thank you for growing with me and I want each of you to know you are a beautiful butterfly, remember regardless of your past or present you are powerful, I'm praying you are transformed and through the process you are set free. It's time for you to find your inner strength and soar.

INTRODUCTION

We all have a story

The roads we travel develop the story God writes for each of us individually, the roads will take you through valleys, storms, trials and tribulations.

Remember there is a divine plan and a purpose to what you experience. If you are struggling, take comfort in knowing you are never alone. While reading I hope the testimonies will minister to you, encourage you, and inspire you to keep pressing forward through this journey of life with your full armor of God on. See how God can take a lost, broken soul that has surrendered to him to a new higher level in life, experience the transformation that only God can do.

TABLE OF CONTENTS

Chapter 1: Words are Powerful

Death and life are in the power of the tongue.

Isaiah 53:4-54 *Surely, he took up our pain and bore our suffering, yet we considered him punished by God, stricken by him, and afflicted. 5 But he was pierced for our transgressions, he was crushed for our iniquities; the punishment that brought us peace was on him, and by his wounds we are healed.*

Sometimes we wonder why we were created by God, was it for us to go through the many trials and tribulations we endure? I found myself asking this question a lot as I found myself trying to figure out who am I, and what was I created for? Growing up I lived a middle-class lifestyle, both of my parents raised me and my siblings, money never seemed like an issue whatever we asked for we received as long as we were obedient. My father was a giver, material things were his prize and his way of expressing love. I can remember a time in Far Rockaway, NY when it was extremely cold my father went and bought me and my sister a fur coat to attend an event. He wanted us to look our best, but the material assets, trips and luxury were at a cost, our lifestyles on the outside were admired but at home I was missing something. Don't get me wrong my father loved us but also wanted us to live successful lives. His peculiar way of discipline caused me to be insecure, unsure of myself and always looking for his validation.

My mother always instilled in us we can become anything in life if we put our mind to it, growing up she would always share with me the trauma she endured during my birth, so I will be reminded of God's love and purpose in my life. My mother wanted me to know I was a blessing, when she went into labor the enemy intended to destroy me in the womb and end her life, somehow the placenta went in front of me and the umbilical cord wrapped around my neck. This caused my mother to hemorrhage, due to the large amount of blood lost she slipped into a slight coma and I was not breathing when I was delivered, my circulation was cut off from the umbilical cord, so the doctors immediately went to work upon my arrival, needless to say God prevailed in our lives. My mom always said I was not only a blessing to her but to this world, God has an assignment on my life that will impact and change the world I am a miracle.

My father was retired military so some of his discipline tactics and chosen words were instilled in him from his military career, one that changed the way I viewed my abilities to have a successful school career and adult life was anytime I misbehaved or did anything he disapproved off I would constantly hear "You are not going to amount to shit" this rip through me like a knife. In my dad's mind this was reverse psychology, the more he said it somehow the words will sink in and I will perform above my abilities while obtaining a life of excellence. Instead I began to believe the words that were spoken to me, as they came out of my father's mouth they began to change the way I thought of myself. I began to see myself as a failure and believed I will not accomplish much in life so there was no need to work hard.

What you think you become, your thoughts have great influence on your life. So, get them working in your favor.

The things you've convinced yourself you cannot do, you will not do. By the same token, whatever you're absolutely certain that you can accomplish you will certainly accomplish.

Your thoughts directly and persistently control your actions. And through your actions, you create much of the reality of your life.

Every achievement begins with a thought. And every achievement is supported all along the way by a continuous flow of positive, empowering thoughts.

You won't make something happen just by thinking about it. Yet the things you do cause to happen are those things upon which your thoughts are steadily focused.

Fill your mind with thoughts of positive purpose, joy, and meaningful achievement. Let your thoughts lead the way to a life filled with God's purpose and will, a life you can only dream of.

Someone should have reminded me how important it was to love thy self, to not look to others for your life's purpose. I know my father intended for those words to empower me, his thoughts were I would embrace them and they would provide the fire I needed to never settle for average. Unfortunately, it did not work for me and I began to fill the void by any means necessary, friends became my source of empowerment. The more friends I had the more my self-esteem grow, regardless if they were good or bad, I began to find myself in circles I did not belong.

I craved acceptance from everyone, in high school I always wanted everyone to like me. Depending on who I was seeking acceptance from I would do things like doing their homework, carrying books, trying out for sports because others wanted me to, skipping class, bring people lunch all so that others I surrounded myself with will see the importance of me in their lives. I needed someone to tell me I was great and irreplaceable, I wanted them to confide in me, seek me for advice with life issues, boy issues, school issues whatever bothered them I wanted to fix it then I will feel complete.

I just wanted to be accepted by everyone. Instead of having them accept me for who I was, I allowed them to change me into who they thought I should be.

There were times I would sit in my room crying because I knew there was an event that some peers at school would be attending and I was not invited. My bedroom window faced the road that was at the entrance and exit of my community. I would sit at the window and watch as friends would be piled in the car to attend the very event I was not invited to, I began to feel as if one-day people would not accept me anymore.

Being accepted made me feel happy, but I always wanted more. I thought it was impossible that someone would like me forever, or need me in their life forever. I was scared that one day I would wake up alone, no one would value my presence or friendship and the words I feared would be a reality.

You are the average of the five people you spend the most time with. You must be 100% all in with everything you do in life, focus on your "WHY", focus on the necessary steps it will take to achieve your goals. Forget what others spoke over your life, forget what others said was impossible for you, what others said you would not accomplish and focus on what could be, for your future and your family. Most obstacles melt away when we make the decision to walk through them.

Your soul is designed to allow you to soar, your brain keeps you safe, so it reminds you of your past, it reminds you of any negative words or action in your life that will keep you bound up. But when you get to the edge you must quiet your brain and listen to your soul and jump to victory. We have to always remember to guard our hearts, eyes, ears and mind from negative thoughts and experiences taking roots and holding us captive against our will.

Somehow, I gathered up enough strength after several disappointments to convince myself I had what it takes to be successful, I was beautiful, and I did not need validation from anyone. Life can be messy. Slowly you learn to hide the mess inside, where no one else can see. Just you and don't forget to put a big smile on your face, people are watching.

My thoughts were in order for life to be meaningful and worthwhile, it had to be like a fairy tale. I began to get involved in church activities and became more focused on my school work, repeating to myself one day I will be someone.

I began to listen to the words taught at church and put my trust in Jesus, to help me. Despite this, I had a lot of lust, emotional chaos, pride and fear that were so rooted in me and I was able to hide it all from everyone. I figured I had everything under control and could balance my feelings and this dark thought life with a very bright outward life. I formed a resume of great achievements, activities, sports and Jesus to prove I had it all together.

How many times do we go through life staying in the dark, we have access to the power of prayer, but we refuse to use it in our daily lives.

Prayer is the fundamental key to successful living, where you bring heaven to earth. Prayer can also create newness in your life, renewing your mind body and soul. Soon my high school career would end, and the real test of life would begin, how long could I guard my heart and mind of the dark thoughts and feelings that have been buried deep within the layers of my perfect appearance.

There is so much power in the words we speak, as it written in Proverbs 18:21 (KJV), Death and life are in the power of the tongue: and they that love it shall eat the fruit thereof. What we say today creates our tomorrow, if we want a healthy and prosperous future then we need to use wisdom and speak words that bring positive results. Our future depends on it.

Chapter 2: PAIN IS NOT LOVE

Love is not what hurts you, someone that doesn't know how to love hurts you.

Love is patient, love is kind. It does not envy, it does not boast, it is not proud. It does not dishonor others, it is not self-seeking, it is not easily angered. It keeps no record of wrongs.

Love does not delight in evil but rejoices with the truth. It always protects, always trusts, always hopes, and always perseveres.

New beginnings are always an exciting and fearful experience, I remember the first day I walked onto an unknown campus where everyone and everything was unfamiliar.

I thought to myself this is an opportunity to show everyone how successful I will become and make my father extremely proud of me, I will be honest it was a little intimidating seeing all the dorms and people walking around on campus.

As I gathered all my belongings out of the vehicle, I was excited to meet new people who have some of the same interests as me. Meeting my new professors that will help me become successful inside and outside the classroom, my parents always told me they wanted me to be better than them especially my father.

Embarking on this new chapter in my life is not only going to be fun and exciting but I will be able to learn my individual responsibility and independence. Most of the time as teenagers we all say I can't wait to leave the house and move on to college, the military, trade school or whatever else you choose after high school. We are finally away from our parent's rules and regulations, telling us what to do and when to do it, then I began to think who will prepare my meals, who will do my laundry. Then I realized this is my opportunity to find a place I belonged and not depend on others for validation, so I thought.

I might be small framed, but a girl can eat so when I heard a knock on my dorm door inviting me to join the other new students at the welcome banquet, my soul began to sing.

Walking into the cafeteria that was transformed nicely by upper classmates and staff was a beautiful touch.

The aroma of different dishes was captivating, and I was ready to eat, as I patiently waited in line I peeked over the crowd to get a glimpse at my menu choices.

I was not a big vegetable fan so as I made my food choices I walked right past that section, then I heard a sweet strong voice say you did not get any vegetables. I turned around surprised and asked were you talking to me, this tall light skinned clean cut guy with a Latin accent walked closer and said yes, a pretty girl like you should eat her vegetables.

I could not help but to smile from ear to ear, I started to get this weird squirmy feeling in my stomach. I was never allowed to date before so the mere fact that this random guy thought enough of me to suggest I make healthy choices left a smile on my face the rest of the evening.

A couple of days went by and my roommate told me there was a guy on campus trying to figure out who I was, I knew it had to be my vegetable guy. Walking to my dorm one day I ran into him, as I passed him he grabbed my hand and pulled me close to him. I can feel my stomach knotting up, I didn't know what was happening to me I began to stutter and get confused.

Thinking to myself what has come over me, this is stuff you see in the movies, his brown eyes made my heart skip a beat for I had never seen or felt anything so breathtaking.

All of this was new to me I was only 17, I was inexperienced and naive; I thought that there was no heart break in love. We spent months getting to know each other, our conversations were filled with laughter, and moments of silence when we just stared at each other.

We became inseparable, he would look deep into my eyes while holding my face in the palm of his hands and tell me my life was with him, my thoughts became his, I was his world and I didn't even know it.

I finally had someone who thought the world of me, could not live without me, shared the same air as me. I was on cloud nine, I was willing to give him every part of me and I did, we planned a camping trip for our anniversary and that weekend changed my life forever.

I thought I was in love and he cared so much about me, I was willing to share everything with him but what did that mean. My emotions were like a foreign country to me, the language my body was speaking was indescribable. See I grew up in a household with strict culture and rules encounters with the opposite sex was non-existing.

Growing up I lived a sheltered life, meaning a lifestyle where I was protected too much from experiencing things. Most of my peers began to go out on group dates at the age of sixteen that was unheard of in my household. Boys were not even allowed to call my house, but I was clever there was this amazing telephone feature called 3-way calling.

I would have one of my female friends call my house to speak to me and have a boy from school on the line I had a crush on, so we could talk. My dad was old school and up on "game" as he called it, so he would periodically in silence pick up the phone and listen to my conversations, so the 3-way trick ended quickly along with my phone privileges.

My dad was adamant about keeping us pure and his girls not bringing no babies into his house without a husband to the point he would periodically take us to the family doctor to get a general checkup, but every visit had an underlying purpose if it was my father accompanying us to the appointment.

There was vital information each visit providing that allowed us to remain on my father's good side as well as the checkbook to stay open. At each visit we would get the normal checkup then a special look at us was requested to ensure everything was still in its proper place and we remained virgins.

Needless to say, my sheltered childhood keeps me from experiencing things other girls my age were experiencing. I had very little involvement in things I thought would be exciting like group dates, teenage parties, group sleepovers, being dropped off at friends' houses, etc. My rope was held on tight, in order to keep me focused on my school work and future.

Unfortunately, that rope left me curious and wanting to break that rope into a million pieces, so I can experience what I thought was fun and live life, especially after leaving the boundaries of my parents' home to attend school.

That weekend I decided to remove all the boundaries that were put on me by my dad and be free to fall into the arms of this guy that had my stomach in knots, an uncontrollable smile on my face, and my heart with flutters every time he stared at me. I always dreamed of what it felt like to walk the hallways and hold hands with someone I loved, giggle for no reason when you see that special someone walk past, day dream about your future life with the one you thought was Mr. Perfect. I finally experienced that, and it was no day dream, it was my reality and that night I gave myself in the name of love.

My weekend was kind of unexpected, so for a few days I was feeling like I can't believe that happened. Sex is an emotional thing and should not be taken lightly, when you decide to allow yourself to connect with someone who is not your spouse in a sexual encounter you allow yourself to have a soul tie with this individual. We read about this in Genesis 34: 2-3, 2. And when Shechem the son of Hamor the Hivite, prince of the country, saw her, he took her, and lay with her, and defiled her. 3. And his soul clave unto Dinah the daughter of Jacob, and he loved the damsel, and spake kindly unto the damsel.

This is why it is so common for a person to still have feelings towards an ex-lover even years down the road. A person may still think of someone they were intimate with, you begin to develop certain characteristics that are uncommon to you all because of a soul tie!

The bible speaks of what is known today as soul ties. In the bible, it doesn't use the word soul tie, but it speaks of them when it speaks about souls being knit together, becoming one flesh. A soul tie can serve many functions, but in its simplest form, it ties two souls together in the spiritual realm.

I became spiritually connected to my first love and was unaware of what happened to me. We found ourselves inseparable, we became each other's worlds, we closed everyone around us out and we created our own life where it seemed like only the two of us existed. We had a new-found love, spending every hour of the day together whether in person or on the phone. We were consumed by what we called love.

There was an immediate need for someone to see me and know I was not ready for my childhood to be overtaken with an adult lifestyle, someone I could talk to, confide in, that would not be judgmental. I needed advice, my life was about to drastically change, I found myself seventeen and pregnant.

I woke up feeling a little weird, my mood was different, things didn't smell right. This was nothing like anything I experienced with my cycle. I was still in denial that just a week ago I took a pregnancy test and it gave me a positive result.

Out of fear I kept that news to myself, fear of losing someone that finally showed me how important I was in their life, someone who needed me and could not live without me. I didn't want some silly test to change my possible fate of a fairy tale life with a happy ever after. Suddenly all that changed when I left my dorm room to head to the cafeteria for breakfast. I can see my boyfriend already grabbed a table and was waiting on me to join him, as I waited in line I began to feel a little light headed.

The closer I got to picking out my food the more the smell of a cafeteria full of orange juice began to make my throat itch and my stomach began to flutter but not in a good way. As I approached the entrance to the buffet, the orange juice smell became unbearable and I began to vomit uncontrollably, as I ran outside trying to cover my mouth. My boyfriend runs outside after me, looking disgusted and unaware of what was going on.

As he gently rubbed my back, he pulled my hair back out of my face and asked me Mami are you OK? I began to shake my head no, with watery eyes the next words that came out of his mouth would change our worlds forever. He softly said are you pregnant? Scared to death to answer, I looked up with tears running down my face and said YES!

He immediately grabbed and embraced me tight for what felt like a century not letting go. My fears began to ease knowing that the news of becoming a father did not make him run but my biggest fear still had to be tackled. The thought of telling my parents the perfect image of my future that had been painted for me so adequately had been tainted by my need to be accepted and free to make choices for myself.

The thought of merely my father's disappointing face had me shaking in my boots. I looked at myself in the mirror and said, boy Martha you really messed up now. You are supposed to set an example for your two younger siblings how are going to be able to keep them out of trouble if you can't even stay on the straight and narrow in your own life.

I went over how I would approach my parents several times and nothing seemed to be right. I wanted to do it in a way that maybe it would not hurt so bad or leave permanent damage to my father's heart. I didn't want him to remember this moment in our lives as a time where he lost his precious Martha. We had a joke growing up about my father being like an elephant because he never forgot anything. If you went to tell him something you better have your story right, because believe me the information you share will come back around at a later time.

After much thought, I decided to write a letter to my parents apologizing about my decisions and getting myself pregnant. After several days my mother called me and had a lengthy conversation, at the end she expressed her love for me and she will support me. My father was a totally different story he was hurt and disappointed.

The news pierced my father's heart like fiery arrows, I remember his first thoughts were no it's a joke she is not pregnant. He went through his moments of disappointment, anger and ultimately feelings of failure. He felt like all of the dreams he had for me had been destroyed the night I decided to engage in adult activities. My future was shattered like broken glass in his eyes, a moment of pleasure had stolen my future and changed everything.

I struggled with what my next move would be, I went back and forth whether I was going through with pregnancy or if I was having an abortion. I wasn't the type of girl society puts on abortion posters, my family life did not fit the normal criteria for a teen mom. Most of the young girls getting pregnant in 97 was from single parent homes, lived on certain sides of towns and had limited income, I didn't want anyone to find out my secret. I didn't want to become the next hot topic, I was young scared and just wanted to end it all, returning to my normal life filled with laughter, going out with friends, school and even test was much better than this reality.

I simply didn't understand the value of life as I do now, everyone left the decision up to me. My father made it clear that I needed to figure out what my plans were, the one thing for certain was I was not allowing this unplanned pregnancy to stop me from finishing school. He bluntly said you and that pissy tail boy that got you pregnant need to come up with a plan that does not include you getting stuck with the baby or dropping out of school.

I was only seventeen, no stable job, first year away from home attending school and didn't want to depend on my parents to raise my child. What else was I supposed to do, having an abortion seemed like my only option. I was all over the place with my thoughts I didn't know what was best for me and my future.

It was not an easy decision to make, if I have an abortion than I will probably deal with regret and emotional issues. What if something physically went wrong, I heard of abortions damaging your future chances of having children. On the other hand, if I went through with the pregnancy how would I support my child and myself? Would my boyfriend really stick with me?

All of these things rattled around in my head for weeks, I cried myself to sleep because I was angry that I was stupid enough to allow this to happen. Scared because regardless of which decision I make my life was going to be affected in a huge way, at that moment everything became so real to me.

I always knew my life was important and had purpose, there were many things my parents felt are important for young people to obtain: school, good grades, sports and accomplishments. I did not know how to fit teen mom in that vision, after I made my final decision to have an abortion I remember sitting in the doctor's office and a woman started to randomly speak to me.

Where do you see yourself one or two years from now is what she asked me moments after we began speaking to each other, I was so emotional about the process I was about to endure I could barely speak to her. She asks me another question what is important to you right now? Her reply, your child of course is most important. Your unborn child thinks you are important. You are going to be a great mother, it will not be easy, but the good news is that you're up to the journey.

Sweetheart motherhood is going to teach you more about yourself than you ever expected. You'll work harder than you ever have before, you'll prove you're strong and capable, the care you will give your child will be nourishing and beneficial to the future. Love is the most important ingredient when it comes to parenting, love as you will discover can help you to achieve the impossible and you will. As she raised up out of her chair to stand up so did I, she had the most beautiful smile on her face as she leaned in to embrace me with a hug.

I never got the chance to tell her I was having an abortion, I just realized she was sent there to remind me of the beautiful gift I was carrying. Even if it came at an unexpected time and not under perfect circumstances it still was a beautiful gift that is not returnable.

I wiped the tears off of my face, went to the restroom to clean my face and searched for my mother. When I found her, I hugged her so tight and told her me and her grandchild was ready to go home. She looked at me with a big ol' grandma grin and said are you sure sweetheart, I nodded my head yes and said I'm tired of worrying about what others will say or think, yes I'm pregnant, yes I'm only seventeen, but I'm going to let my baby live and learn to be a great mother. She grabbed my hand and said let's go home. Before getting pregnant I hadn't thought much about what I wanted to do with my life, except that I'd considered being a counselor and hoped to be married with three to five children someday.

After getting pregnant, I struggled with the thought of how I would make everything work becoming a mother but still reaching a high level of success as a professional. I began to think it was no use to hold on to those dreams because I messed up and taking care of my child had to become my first priority.

It would have been easy for me to just give up and not try. I'm thankful that I dared to work hard to achieve my goals; with an amazing support team and my parents being my number one cheerleaders I was able to be a mom and become a counselor.

Me and my boyfriend said the happiest day of our lives was when our son was born, we began to build this life together and a day would not go by that he did not thank me for choosing life for his son.

I was living a dream with my little family, just the three of us against the world. It was everything I wanted, I had completely moved into my role as mother and wife. Finally, what I thought was happiness seemed to finally be a reality in my life.

One of the funniest lines I ever heard about dating was something comedian Chris Rock once said: "When you date, have you ever noticed when you meet somebody for the first time you're not meeting them. You're meeting their "representative". Then after about three months you meet the real candidate".

This statement is hilarious, but every word is true, only for me the real candidate began to be revealed about the second year. I came from a line of strong women who voice their opinion, naturally I developed this trait maybe too well for my son's father taste. If I did not agree with something, I would let it be known and expect my opinion to be respected.

My family adored him and was always complementing my son's father for the way he cared for his family. I did have one aunt though, that would ask me periodically am I ok she began to see something in him that I couldn't see. I would usually say he just has a little temper it's no big deal, we were Bonnie and Clyde, Will and Jada, it was us against the world. Because I love him, and he loved me I will just endure.

One day we were in the living room and I remember I was holding my son rocking him while we had a discussion. At some point the conversation became hostile because I was not in agreeance of the plans, it was his way or the highway. I wanted and needed to have some kind of input on the decision making and I made that perfectly clear. That day was the first time he slapped me, the impact was so intense while holding my son I fell back onto the couch and flipped over onto the floor. I grabbed my son so close to my body, holding him tight while protecting him using my body as a shield, I didn't know what would happen next.

At that moment I was confused and in shock, how can someone who says they love me turn around and hurt me? He left the house for hours, when he returned he immediately began to apologize and hand me red roses. My favorite color, I was happy to have these roses that I forgot about the pain in my face and body. Needless to say I accepted the gift and his apology.

I began to tell myself he didn't mean to hurt you and he will never hit you again. Boy how wrong was I, over the next year he began to drink and became more violent. Sometimes he could not even remember his actions. When I would ask him why he was hurting me that caused him to become angrier because he could not remember his actions. He would punch me, slap me and push me into objects. I didn't tell anyone about the abuse.

I was embarrassed, and I didn't want anyone to say, you made another mistake, so I just dealt with the painful abuse and reminded myself that he always said I love you more than life. He would say; you know no one is going to love you like I love you, you are all I got and I'm not going to lose you. I would hype myself up to convince my mind I can handle the abuse, I will be fine he loves me. Mentally, you become so messed up that you start to think you are part of the problem.

We stayed together for several years the cycle would go like this, abuse, apology, forgiveness, gifts, change for the better and repeat the cycle from the beginning all over. I became so immune to the abuse that It was normal for me, everything became numb my feelings and body. Abuse became my drug, something was wrong with me if it didn't happen. I didn't go around family much during this time to avoid any kind of judgment if they found out.

One night we attended a little get together at my oldest sister house, my nieces and nephews were so excited to see me. We all were taking shots of Patron (a strong tequila), laughing, and acting silly just having a great time.

My sister began talking to my son's father about a specific topic and they were having a detailed dialogue. When she turned to me and said Martha what do you think? I was excited to share my thoughts, I began by saying you both have great view points but let's look at this situation a different way. I begin to explain my point of view and he interrupts me and say so are you saying I'm incorrect? In love, I looked at him and said no honey I just see things differently and he yelled out, so you are disagreeing with me? I didn't like his tone of voice, so I immediately said no love, you are absolutely correct.

He slowly and silently got up with a blank face and said I will be right back, knowing him at this point I should have been on guard and aware of his emotional shift and body language. He abruptly returned with a chef's knife that he threatened me with, as I quickly tried to get up I stumbled to the floor. Keeping my arms up guarding my face in order to protect myself from anything he does with the knife, as I swiftly crawled backwards he chased me backing me up into a corner of the wall. With so much anger and hatred in his voice he said stand up, he held the knife to my throat pressing it against esophagus until I began to feel little drops of blood roll down my neck.

In this moment I felt like something in me broke physically and mentally, my knees began to buckle as he continued to use the knife to forcefully hold me against the wall. As I begun to feel weak, I closed my eyes and asked God to spare my life, I silently cried and prayed to God if you get me out of this situation I will leave and never look back. I knew I had to get out of this safely, one wrong move and he would have slit my throat killing me. My sister was able to calm him down long enough that I was able to slip away. I have never run so fast in my life, I skipped many steps as I leaped down three flights of steps, I didn't care if I fell, or broke my ankle I just needed to get out of that house. I busted out the front door and the iron gate leading to the front door, I heard a voice behind me say Martha.

I was so terrified I didn't even turn around, I just ran like my life depended on it two blocks in the New York cold air to my apartment building. I ran into my apartment, I had every piece of furniture in front of all the doors, so he could not get in the apartment. For the first time, I was brave enough to seek help he tried to break in, my son's father was banging on the outside gate to get to our front door and throwing rocks at the windows. He attempted to pry open the gate with a crowbar my sister gave him, I remained quiet in the house crying my soul out.

That night I believe he had every intention on killing me, I was terrified, broken, scared and abused. I fell into a deep sleep, when I woke up the next morning, I looked at myself in the mirror trying to figure out how did I get here. How did I allow this relationship to get this bad? Whatever the answer is I knew I had to take action quickly.

I made a necessary phone call to my mother, crying I said me and Antonio need to come stay with you for a while. I can hear my dad asking what's wrong, my mother sent the money needed for a one-way ticket. Within three hours I had efficiently packed whatever could fit in our suitcase and grabbed a cab to the Greyhound station.

I could not believe my fairy tale was ending in such a tragic way, how did I miss the signs, what happened to I love you more than life. It was all a lie that I believed and was willing to give my life for.

Looking back, I wish I had sought help if not from my family and friends, then from someone else. I now know that no matter how it feels, you are never alone. You can break free if you trust yourself.

Chapter 3: Broken

Because your actions speak the truth. I trusted you, but now your words mean nothing to me.

When you've been in an abusive relationship, opening yourself up to love again is a consistent uphill battle. You want to trust and love again, but you can't help but worry that you'll fall for another manipulative controlling type. While it's easy to fall back into the same old pattern, you're entirely capable of breaking it. For several years, I spent time healing my wounds I developed a lot of self-esteem issues during that toxic relationship that I was able to work through.

I was on a mission to soul search, figure out who I was and what I was supposed to be doing with my life. I began to travel the world see and experience different cultures, finally I was like a bird free without limitations. When I made the decision to let go of my fears, and allow my hurts to empower me instead of keeping me trapped as a victim.

It certainly wasn't the right time for me to take off and travel when I was still getting through the emotional and mental damages of enduring a violent relationship. I used to travel with my parents yearly and went to several destinations with my ex, but never did I even think to jump on a plane or ship by myself.

After spending several years learning to love myself and become a better mother and know who I was as a woman. When I told my friends and mother my plans, they all thought it was a bad idea, they wanted me to stay home, finish building my career and stick to my plan of rebuilding my life. I had just bought a house two years prior for me and my son, I understand why everyone didn't want me to go but I'm thankful I decided not to listen and follow my heart.

I'm thankful my parents believe in me enough to allow me the freedom to find happiness within. I learned to sit with my grief and uncomfortable feelings, to trust myself to make good decisions and trust my instincts and to be open to the possibilities of love and a different way of living my life.

After several of my solo voyages I was a completely different woman, the new and improved version of me felt confident, free, independent, trusting of myself, and the world around me. I spent three years soul searching, getting to know myself and developing self-love. I felt I was ready to find the love I knew was possible for me and determined to create a life I loved, instead of adapting to a version of life someone else created for me.

I grew and healed more during those trips more than I ever had in years of therapy and survivor groups. It was amazing to see myself return healed and ready to create an amazing life for me and my son, I changed in ways beyond the reaches of anything that I could accomplish in my therapy sessions.

I remember one visit to the airport I was walking on the lower level of the airport right outside baggage claim, for whatever reason it was extremely busy that day. As I continued my journey, I waited for the enterprise courtesy van to pick up passengers from the rental car stop, so I could pick up my rental vehicle. On that short ride, I met a nice gentleman who would become my best friend, we exchanged numbers to keep in touch. He seemed like a down to earth cool guy, after several days we were in contact, our conversation was enlightening.

I remember a time that I enjoyed speaking to him so much we had a set time that we both were free. I would look at the clock and as the time grew near prepare for my phone call, I would wait and then quietly grab a cup of tea and a comfy blanket, find a soft spot on my couch and curl up on the couch. Then my phone would ring and for hours into the night me and my best friend would talk, we would share hours and hours of conversation. We revealed secrets to each other, talked about our past hurts, he expressed to me how broken he was when his ex-girlfriend he was building a life and family with became pregnant and later he found out the life he was building was a lie because the baby was not his. His mother and sister helped him gather all his belongings and he just fell out in despair, sadness, and became overwhelmed with tears, anger and a broken heart.

I gave him advice from a female perspective on dating with purpose, and being honest if you choose to date multiple women at the same time. I shared with him the many dark days I endured in my abusive relationship, he was shocked that someone could not see how precious and valuable I was and not treasure that. These were the type of conversations that built our two-year friendship and kindled a slow burning fire, but just as quickly as I can summarize our friendship in one sentence that is how quickly things in life can change.

Fast forward a year, during one of our many conversations we had the talk. You know that talk that you have when you are just friends but everything you do together says relationship. I mean but I am the woman you confide in about other women; how can we possibly entertain the thought of a relationship. On the other hand, I know him and all his secrets so there is nothing to worry about, right?

Never get mad at someone for being who they've always been, be upset with yourself for not coming to terms with it sooner. This is a lesson I learned time and time again. I am a loving, loyal, and big-hearted person, the moment I learned to live my life from the point of truth I could survive anything.

Being a best-friend and a spouse were two totally different roles to play. Even though it was a scary thought we decided to get married, even after he cancelled the first wedding (that alone should have been a red flag) we scheduled, planned and paid for. Now instead of knowing all the secrets I became the secret not knowing the true life I was living with no knowledge. I was about to go on a roller coaster ride I didn't choose too, or have the proper restraints to ride safely. We moved into a new house and quickly began creating new traditions, like seafood Fridays, out to eat Saturdays and super soul food Sundays. We were beginning to live the American dream as I knew it, you know careers, house with a white picket fence. The type of family life we seen growing up on our favorite sitcoms.

One night we had movie night, and he told me he was going to hang out with his boys, I asked him to watch a movie with his family first prior to heading out. He ends up falling asleep on the couch instead of going out, late that evening his phone dinged to alert him he had received a text message. I figured it was his friend he was supposed to hang out with so as I opened his phone to let his friend know he fell asleep, to my surprise it was not the friend I was told he would be hanging out with.

I quickly snapped a photo of the text with the girl name and number then quietly placed his phone back exactly as he had it. There was not enough time to scroll all through the messages, to get a clear understanding of their history. I kept quiet about the text I read, as I continued with life as normal just allowing everything to soak in. I needed time to process this information, as the sun rise, and my husband began to get ready for work; I sent him off with a sarcastic statement. Don't do anything I wouldn't do and have a great day.

I waited until I knew he was at work and was done with the daily morning meeting, then I called the landline phone at his office instead of his cell phone to ensure he was at work. When he answered the phone call, I greeted him with hi honey just wanted to make sure you made it to work safely.

After I hung up the phone I immediately went into detective mode, I called the number listed on the text to ask questions. I did not want to automatically blame the other women, but I needed her to tell me who she was and what kind of relationship she was having with my husband.

As I dialed her number the phone just rung until the voice-mail came on, I just hung up. After a couple of minutes, she called back, I answered the phone and she said to me; hello did you just call? I answered yes, I did. As the conversation continues she begins to tell me she did not know he was married, they have been seeing each other for a short period about three weeks. The night he fell asleep, he was supposed to come over and have a Netflix and chill kind of evening, she went on to share with me he was just over there the other day spending time with her and I should be relieved because he was a good boy. There was nothing else to discuss with her, she gave me everything I needed before hanging up I told her now that you are aware he is married I suggest you stay away from my husband.

I could not be mad at her, she said he didn't tell her

he was married so my issue was with the man I took vows with. This woman did not owe me loyalty, but I made it very clear with the right adult words that if she continued to have a relationship with my husband after our conversation there would be serious consequences. The funny thing is I didn't feel anything like sadness, anger, or no visible tears I just wanted revenge. All I wanted was to make him pay for the mistake he made, I didn't expect him to be completely honest about cheating.

Remember I was his best friend before his wife, I knew him better than he knew himself. These conversations were familiar to me the only difference now was I was his wife dealing with other women, not his best friend coaching him to be honest to the multiple women he was seeing. After several conversations, I decided to just forgive him, I mean after all they did not have sex yet; even though that was the plan the night he fell asleep according to the woman he was seeing.

I'm not blind to the fact that a husband cheating is something that can happen to anyone, however I never thought I would have to deal with confronting other women especially from him. It did not matter to me that the same behavior I saw as his best friend was evident in my marriage. I always told myself I was different, he would never treat me like those other girls I'm his wife!

When I found those text messages and found out he had been seeing another woman for several weeks, I found it a bitter pill to swallow.

Our family we had built was the most important thing to us both, so we both vowed to avoid distractions and outside influences in our marriage. Time went by and we were back on track trying to love each other like spouses are supposed to love each other, the children seemed to be happier as well. We began to play with each other again like elementary school kids at recess, we were having fun with life again and our marriage. Smiling, laughing, joking with each other, then I began to get these feelings like Mayweather punched me in my stomach.

I went to several doctors because the pain in my stomach was so intense, I did not know what was wrong with me. They could not find a problem either, and they concluded it could be caused by stress. I had no idea things were not in order as much as I thought they were, of course I had some suspicions that he was deceiving me, and I began to see his behavior as well as his feelings change. To fix whatever my husband was lacking I attempted to make much more effort to please him and make him happy. I went out of my way to learn new things and dress more seductive, I felt like this would help get things on track.

I have always been confused with trying to understand the logic behind having an affair for an extended period is an easier thing to achieve than it is to simply talk to the woman you married and became one with in front of God about your feelings. My feelings that something wasn't right were confirmed when I looked for reassurance by going through his phone again. I never wanted to turn into the type of wife that is caught snooping in her husband's phone but when something is such a big part of your life and future it is understandable to do so.

As I went back to his phone to confront him about the messages, magically they were deleted. I was furious knowing that the evidence had been destroyed, with him I must bring proof when asking him about infidelity or he will deny it. I needed a break from all this madness, so I decided to go on a weekend getaway with one of my friends, we brought our children and her mother. She rented a vehicle big enough that we all fit so we only need one vehicle, I needed this getaway, so I can clear my head and truly look at my life like I never have before.

Atlanta was hot, but we were having a blast regardless of the heat. We went to College Park, Stone Mountain, Duluth County and metro Atlanta. We wanted to experience Atlanta like a tourist, my friend's mom received a phone call from her associate pastor reminding her to arrive at church early on Sunday. She agreed even though we were out of town.

Mrs. Jones my friends mother asked if it was ok to leave Sunday but very early, so she could arrive at church by 9am for 11am service. Originally, we should have been back home around 9pm Sunday, when we returned it was around 6am by the time we drove through town and my friend dropped me and the kids off at my house it was 7am. My car was still parked in the driveway, I entered my home and told the kids to be quiet in case my husband was sleeping. We were exhausted, as everyone carried their bags upstairs I had them get ready for bed.

I went to go let my husband know I was home, surprisingly he was not in our room. I went to check the garage to see if his car was there, when I didn't see his car there either I was tempted to call but my instincts stopped me. I just showered and put on some cute night clothes, even though I didn't confront him about the messages and possible infidelity before I left, I wanted to engage in adult activity. He still was my husband, I missed him, and a girl has needs you know, in this moment Mr. Dependable was just not going to get the job done.

I dozed off and on in sleep, until loud voices woke me up. I realized it was my husband he was home, I sat up in the bed and posed to make myself look appealing when he walked into the bedroom. As he walked further into the house, I can begin to clearly hear his conversation. The calmness and openness to have such a conversation was because in his mind he was alone, his family was still in Atlanta and it was an open play field. As I remained completely still so I would not alert him of my presence, I can hear a soft voice on the other end say; are you sure your family is still out of town? My husband replies yes, they won't be home until tomorrow, she replies ok great I really think you are sexy.

As she began to explain in detail all the different things she will perform on him sexually, my mind is still stuck on her asking was your family still out of town. At this point my blood is boiling, not only are you sleeping with my husband, but you are knowingly disrespecting my house and my marriage, I'm going to kill them both. I can hear the excitement in his voice increase with every word spoken, he begins to give her the address and directions to our home. The more I listened, it was like someone had placed their hands around my throat and began choking me.

Tears began to rapidly run down my face, I tried to open my mouth to speak but words would not come out. I felt like someone had just took a knife and stabbed me right in the heart, my breathing was short, and my vision became blurry. I didn't know what was taking over me, it's funny how having the confirmation of your suspicions (however sure of them you already are) can really knock you off your feet. The realization that this is happening to me, he is my best friend and outside of the infidelity our lives were great. He was a great father, loved to cook, meat on the grill, hard worker, love to clean, overly neat, funny and a diehard eagles fan but he could not love me and only me.

What is wrong with me, I began to ask myself as I heard him walk up the stairs. I can still hear the conversation between the two of them, I had no idea how I would react when he walked into our room. The thought of another woman sleeping with my husband in my bed kept replaying in my head.

As he walked into the room and saw me sitting on the bed with my wet t-shirt from all the tears that ran down my face, he did a double take to make sure his eyes were correct. He developed a startled look on his face like he just saw a ghost, he lost his balance for a quick second and took a step back. As soon as he realized he was really seeing me sitting there in our bed as he was inviting another woman over he immediately hung up the phone and went into a rage.

He began to yell at me, calling me names as I returned the choice words swinging a bat at him ready to bust his head to the white meat. He said I was a liar and set him up, this just added fuel to the fire that was burning inside of me. How was this fool blaming me for his actions, I began to explain why I was home early as I heard his phone ring repeatedly going off it was the other woman calling. I dashed for the phone, I wanted to talk to this heffa. As we fought over the phone, I gained strength and pushed his head into the wall. I was so filled with rage, I wanted to fight him and that heffa, my hands were itching to meet her face.

I began to strike my husband with everything I could find to pick up, the more I hit him the more he spoke words out of his mouth I never thought I would hear from him. I just wanted answers, why? What am I not doing right? What is it that you need? Anything I was in so much pain, the hurt was unbearable. My house, my bed is you out of your damn mind, you and that heffa have a death wish and you both have the right one to grant it.

As I backed him up near the stairs, I can see fear in his face. He knew at that point he had pushed me to a level where my behavior was unpredictable, everything in me wanted to kick him down the stairs until his head hit the wood floor and bust open. I was furious as he ran down the stairs, I ran back into our room throwing everything in our closet on the floor I was searching for something that at the state of mind I was in could change my life forever.

As I found the black box I was looking for, I put the code in opened it and there was a beautiful black 9-millimeter staring me in my face. As I picked it up, I began to run several thoughts through my head. I can hear voices tell me how much better I would feel if I just pull the trigger, he deserved it. If I shoot him I will go to jail, who would take care of my children who slept peacefully in their rooms sound asleep. Unaware of the madness going on in the house, I paced the floor upstairs with the gun in my hands wanting nothing more but to bring my husband pain.

I wanted him to hurt like I hurt, cry like I cried, I wanted him to suffer. I felt like I had flames coming out my ears, I walked to the stairs sat down with both hands holding the gun. One finger on the trigger ready to play Russian roulette with my husband and have no regards of any consequences.

As I sat there for a moment, I felt a calm spirit come over my body. It was like the calm before the storm, I softly called my husband to the stairs. As I began to raise my head with blood shot red eyes and an ashy face from dried tears everything in me wanted to keep pulling the trigger of this gun until the one bullet entered his chest and I saw his body parts and blood exit his body.

Somehow, I believed this would bring me so much peace and help with the pain I was feeling, instead I calmly raised the gun and told him I don't trust my actions with you in my presence, so I need you to leave and not return until I call. He knew this was serious, through everything I have never reacted in this manner or asked him to leave but I needed space to avoid jail time.

I was hurt, you go through so many emotions in that space of time. All the ones you might expect; anger, hate, sadness, fear just a roller coaster of emotion and feelings. I immediately went to the computer to log onto my cell phone account, there I can see the number the woman on the phone called from. Listen when you are a woman scorned you become an FBI agent, I could retrieve the address associated with the number. Somehow, I found myself sitting outside her home. Prior to me taking any action confronting her or anything of that sort I needed to make sure it was her place, I heard another lady call her by name standing in front of her home. I knew I had the right place, I called the only person I knew would be down to fight and get her hands dirty my cousin T, all she needed was a brief description of the problem. She told me not to get out the car until she arrived, driving 90 MPH down the highway she drove a 25-minute route in 10 minutes, her adrenaline was going.

When she arrived, we got out the car, immediately we began destroying the other woman. Her license tag was personalized so we knew which car was hers, we began to call her outside. Her and the other lady looked out the window and did not come outside, said they were calling the police. I told her to bring her coward behind outside, you bold enough to come to my house to have sex with my husband you should be bold enough to come outside and get these hands. I was so furious I wanted to punch her face in, but she would not come outside, I was able to view emails sent to the trash can prior to me arriving to her house.

The visions of all the things she did with my husband that were spelled out in the emails were playing in my head, the more I saw them the angrier I became. I looked down to my side and noticed a loose brick as I heard sirens and my cousin T yelling at me to get in the car, I picked up the brick threw it through her front window and yelled at her you scared Heffa. I jumped in the car and we speed off in the opposite direction of the sirens, hoping not to get caught the last thing I needed was a charge.

I arrived back home and fell out on the floor, screaming crying, kicking the floor, and punching the air. I just needed time to process everything, I acted like an out of control teenager. If I went to jail was this man worth it, I mean we have four children we were responsible for. We built a beautiful house and life together was I just going to allow the other women to come in and snatch that away.

I always dreamed I would be in a marriage that would be stable enough that my children would never experience any kind of parental split, I mean when my father passed my parents were married 35 years. Unfortunately, it looked like my kids would experience this kind of dysfunction.

A couple of days went by and I began to come up with a solution for this madness, if I'm honest with myself I would realize that maybe my husband does love me but he just does not have the ability to be with one woman. I had the perfect solution and needed to call my husband to let him know he should come home. The feelings I had did not disappear with his absence so there was a need to be petty when he returned.

I planned a grand entrance for him, I made dinner, had the house cleaned, smelling good and twenty minutes before he arrived at the front door, I removed any furniture or objects in arm's length. I began to spread four bottles of baby oil over the entire first floor of our home, every inch was saturated I had all the lights off so until you stepped on the floor you could not see the oil. Any door knob that was in the path to the rear of the house was also covered in baby oil, I sat on the stairs to watch it all go down.

As the front door open, I said welcome home I will be right there. As he began to walk on the floor, it was like he was on a slip and slide ride. He fell and bumped his head several times, trying to gain his balance. All I could hear is the vulgar language as I laughed so hard and cried at the same time. He slithered across the floor like a snake, until he reached the stairs I can see visible bruises from his several falls and knocks into the wall. He was saturated in oil and sweat and his three hundred-dollar hard bottoms shoes, he treasured were damaged.

None of that mattered to me because nothing compared to the hurt I was feeling, I asked him to sit on the stairs and gave him the instructions on how we would move forward. I explained how I realized he was incapable of committing to one women, on the same hand I don't want that to destroy our family. My solution was for us to have an open marriage, that way he can continue to be with his women, but our family would not be broken.

He no longer had to worry about keeping secrets, he had to be home every night and no phone calls while in our home. Everything stays outside our home nothing or no one can interrupt our family time. This arrangement news spread like wild flowers through his friends, having all them wishing their wives would agree to the same lifestyle. After a while the thoughts started to sink in that if these arrangements applied to him in an open marriage the same applied to me, the thought of his wife sleeping with another man was unbearable and he decided an open marriage was no longer acceptable.

I was willing to do any and everything to save my marriage and please my husband, so the next arrangement was to open my doors to other women. My husband liked a variety of women, so this was the only other option, it was needed to keep my image of a happy life. If he was happy and satisfied so was I, I tried to find anything that would give him what he needed but also keep my family together.

The threesome idea was all about pleasing him, I set rules me and the other women were not to have physical contact only interact to bring him pleasure. He was not allowed to perform oral sex on another woman, I thought this would give me everything I wanted but instead it made me question my sexuality, feel more insecure, ugly and unwanted. The first time we had a setup and I watched my husband the man I was in love with, the man I stood before God and took vows with, the father of my children, penetrate another woman and get more pleasure from her than I have ever seen him get with me I was broken. It felt like someone took a knife and stabbed me in my heart and chest over and over, I could not show my weakness now, but I realized this was not the answer either, so I ended this arrangement as well.

Clearly, I didn't think once I opened Pandora box it would be that easy to just close it. The different arrangements just opened my husband up to more affairs more often, I reached the point where it was unbearable and we both decided it was time to separate. I helped him search for an apartment, I even helped him move in our discussion regarding this separation was to work on our marriage.

Our goal was to start over, fresh start and begin dating again no one could date or sleep with other people. I went over to his apartment several nights a week to spend the night, wash his clothes, etc. One night I was folding and putting up his laundry, and as I put his underwear in the top drawer I saw a box of condoms.

My heart dropped to the floor, I yelled out so loud come on damnit we are supposed to be working on us no screwing other women. When he came home, I blew up out of anger and he said calm down those belong to my co-worker. I slapped him without even thinking about it and said stop lying, he explained how his co-worker would rent his apartment on his lunch break to sleep with his girlfriend. He could not take her home because he was married, and I'm sure his pregnant wife would not approve.

I began to calm down because I knew this co-worker and knew all about his infidelity, so I told my husband from this day forward let him know he can no longer use your apartment as motel 6. It's not good for our marriage, he agreed and assured me he would handle it so I let it go and we had a great evening dinner.

The following week I was at the dealership where they worked and something in me just wanted to confront my husband co-worker, you know how you get that gut feeling so I trusted my instincts. I asked him did he remove his condoms from my husband's apartment, in so many words and body language he just let me know I caught my husband in a lie. He tried his best to correct himself especially since I caught him off guard with the approach, the more he would try to take the blame for the condoms to protect his boy I just told him to shut up. Once a cheater always a cheater, I patiently waited for my husband to get off work.

I needed answers, I'm sure his co-worker already alerted him, so he was prepared to defend himself. As he walked into his apartment I calmly asked him why did he lie and who is she? Surprisingly I was not mad just tired of the same cycle. I gathered enough strength and nerve needed to talk to him about this truth, I prepared myself for the bold and ugly truth regardless how bad it hurt I was ready to listen. He began to tell me she was a stripper he had met, and he so arrogantly enough said don't worry it was only a fling that meant nothing and at least I wore a condom. As if that would allow me to forgive and forget.

Even a momentary lapse is enough to undo years of love and trust, I felt betrayed. We were rebuilding and regaining our love, his actions changed how our family and future would look from this day forward. At that moment, I concluded that regardless of what I did, how much I loved him it would never be enough for him to just love me. I gave him my all, I loved him past all his faults, I felt like I lost my soul to give him happiness but with all my efforts it was not enough.

I told him that for the sake of a bit more excitement with a stranger you sacrificed your marriage and your family life. I closed my eyes to hold back the tears and took a deep breath, as I opened my eyes I looked at him and grabbed his hands as I kissed him on his cheek. I felt many emotions building up, but things I have been holding onto for years were being released from me. I finally was about to make a decision that would bring me happiness.

While still holding his hands, I starred in his eyes and said I love you, but I love me more. The next words that came out of my mouth would end what I thought was my eternity, I asked for a divorce. I reached in my purse grabbed my keys and removed his apartment keys off my key ring, and placed the keys in his hands. I looked at him and said I hope whatever you are searching for you find it, let's not focus on the downfall of our marriage but build our friendship and co-parent to a point where our children are not affected tremendously.

That night I gained peace, calmness and closure, I was set free.

CHAPTER 4: COVERED BY THE BLOOD

I will never leave you or forsake you. In summer 2008, me and my children left home excited about the day ahead of us. We were singing songs in the car as I drove them to their summer camp destination, I was driving down lawyer's road in Charlotte, NC as I approached the children summer camp I came to a complete stop waiting to make a left turn into the driveway of the camps parking lot.

As I waited to turn I can see my 4-year-old daughter finally figure out how to release her straps on her car seat, she has been attempting this for weeks with no success. She climbs out her car seat down to the floor behind the driver seat, and begins to play with her dolls. As I am watching traffic to see when I can safely turn, I am telling her to get back in the car seat and she would not move.

Suddenly a truck coming behind me does not notice me because right before he came onto Lawyer's road his phone fell into the floorboard of the front passenger seat.

To retrieve his phone, he reached down to pick it up, never placing his foot on the brake. The vehicle reached speeds of 60 MPH, before he knew it he was rear ending my completely stopped vehicle at full speed. The impact hit me so hard it knocked my vehicle into oncoming traffic and another truck T-boned me pushing me into a light pole. Everything went black, I thought I was blind I could not feel my body, I felt blood pouring from every part of my body, my life flashed before my eyes and I remember thinking I don't want to die.

Everything after this point in the natural is what others experienced at the scene. I lost so much blood that I was unresponsive by the time the paramedics arrived. It took several minutes for the ambulance to get there and when they arrived they had to call several more units to assist. The fire department had to use the jaws of life to free me and my children out of this vehicle that had us all twisted up inside of its metal, by this time I had lost several pints of blood, I was barely breathing, my body was lifeless and in shock.

My son had glass that had pierced through the skin of his face, unable to move on his own. He suffered a broken hip bone, broken rib, and bruised lungs. My daughter who suddenly let herself out of her car seat according to the medical staff spared her life by her actions because her car seat ejected out the front window on impact. If she was still buckled in she would have been thrown out the windshield.

The medical staff did everything they could to save my infant son Jayden's life, they did every procedure possible. The impact of both trucks was too much trauma for his body to endure and he lost his life, the severity of the accident caused me to have four brain surgeries, reconstructive surgery on my face, three abdominal surgeries, 25 blood transfusions, leg surgery, I suffered severe brain damage, spinal damage and developed a Chiari Malformation (An opening in my spinal cord, where my brain tissue has now entered).

Due to the impact and trauma I slipped into a coma, unable to breathe on my own I had tubes everywhere in my body including coming out of my skull, during extended time in a coma I had an out of body experience. I knew something was different, because I can see myself laying in the hospital bed. I can hear the doctors give my family my chances of survival report, my spirit had come out of my body and I was hovering over everything that was happening.

Everything my body was enduring, I could not feel I was so peaceful and happy the most joyous feeling ever. I remember walking down the hallway in the hospital, I saw a bright light but this light was like nothing I ever saw before. I can't explain it, this light shined so beautifully I was captivated by the beauty of it, it was gleaming, sparkling and glittering. Then an angel took my hand, I saw beautiful colors and flowers everything was so bright and vibrant in color, I could hear peaceful sounds and as I walked further I saw my grandmother Elizabeth. I attempted to run and hug her, I kept talking to her, but it was like I was speaking to deaf ears. She was not responding, I missed her so much our weekends together. Her baking my favorite chocolate chip cookies, my grandmother was beautiful, no stress in her face, no illness, her hair was so pretty and long.

I can remember there was such a sense of peace and joy, no anger, frustration, worry, race division, all the things on earth was not evident in heaven. Even though my grandmother didn't respond I kept trying to tell her how much I loved her and missed her, how the family is so different now since she left us. I just wanted to feel the warmth of her arms wrapped around me one more time, I was like a lost child scared and needed to feel safe, even though I never got a response being there felt amazing and peaceful. I never wanted to leave, I even saw my little sister that died after I was born right before my parents conceived my baby sister, she was beautiful and resembled my father and grandmother.

I heard a soft voice say to me you cannot stay, it's time for you to return your work is just beginning. I knew at that moment my visit was sadly coming to an end, even though I was not ready to go and return to the tragedy life at dealt me, here I had peace, no sad tears, no pain I begged to stay. I could have more precious moments with my grandmother who my father named me after, it was not fair. What was my purpose for coming here if I had to leave, my angel took me by the hand and lead me back towards that beautiful light. The more I walked forward, the more I felt like a part of me was left behind the image of that beautiful peaceful place was no longer in sight.

I later learned I had stop breathing three times and my heart needed to be jump started to beat again. I was placed on life support the doctors didn't think I would survive, but I have a praying mother and grandmother. They called the ultimate doctor for help, I came out of the coma and eventually started to breath on my own when the doctors had done all they could do and threw in the towel God had to step in and do what man could not do. I went under a total of 20 major surgeries while in the hospital, my family consistently prayed for me by the grace of God I survived and have been healed. I give all glory to the power of prayer and God for my life today.

God has a purpose for my life, that's far greater than my pain and sorrow from this accident or the loss of my son. I could not allow the current tragedy, struggle, accident or recovery to keep me from the blessings God has for me.

CHAPTER 5: DETERMINED

(Be Fearless in the pursuit of what gets your soul on fire)

When God has a purpose for your life, nothing or no one can take your purpose away. Doctor's did not expect me to survive, after enduring several brain surgeries, abdominal surgeries, facial surgeries, spinal surgeries, and going into a coma the doctor delivered life changing news.

He explained to my family the damage was permanent, I had severe brain damage and central nervous system nerve damage. I could not feel anything from the waist down, at most I might get 20 to 50% return. My speech was like speaking with a toddler who was learning new words, family and memories was unfamiliar to me. I lost the ability to do simple things like write with a pencil or read the morning newspaper, my whole world was unfamiliar to me.

The important part for me was realizing I was more than just the circumstances of my mind and body. I just needed to embrace my new way of life and not hold onto what life once was like for me, I needed to create new dreams. My old dreams were shattered, as I left the hospital every type of equipment you can think of went home with me. Portable toilet, hospital bed, wheelchair, pull-up bar, everything that will help me be successful outside of the hospital setting.

When I arrived home, my living room looked exactly like my hospital room I just left just a different location. I even had an in-home physical therapy session corner setup, with a small two drawer dresser to house all the different medications that now became a part of my daily life. Every day I had a schedule for someone to help me eat, bathe, go to the bathroom. Family and friends brought daily meals, sent cards, flowers, text, calls, came by to visit, and left heartfelt voice-mails. I was chauffeured around to my doctor's appointments, and different errands just to get me out the house.

As grateful as I was, I struggled to accept their help. It was always me who was giving, serving and helping others, always in control of my situation, my surroundings and my life. This car accident changed my perspective and humbled my heart, the reality of someone having to wash your private parts as a grown woman was the most humbling experience.

The first day of physical therapy was very

challenging and frustrating at the same time. As my body remained stiff after all my gestures and hard work I began to become angry. Everyone was so focused on the physical injures that we never talked about or began to deal with the emotional injuries as well. After an accident the emotions of shock, anxiety and depression can affect your physical progress, after months of daily physical therapy, speech therapy and interactive therapy there was only a small increase in my abilities.

I still could not hold conversations with people, because I lack the ability to speak clearly. It was so frustrating, I knew exactly what I wanted to say but my brain would not form the words to speak complete sentences. I can remember one day I was so tired of being stuck in the living room, not able to fully access my home that I pushed the wheelchair over in anger used my upper body strength to get out of that hospital bed and scooted my body to the stairs.

I was fed up and feeling sorry for myself, I felt stupid because I could not talk, ugly because all my hair was gone, glass entered my face and damaged my gums, so I have most of my back teeth missing which damaged my smile. I gained weight because of all the medications, I didn't have control of my body anymore. I needed some type of my normal life to return, I was tired of pooping in a toilet that was in the middle of my living room asking for help to wipe afterwards. Waiting on someone to wash me, get me dressed and out of bed, I was tired of this big bulky junk of metal they called a wheelchair. I became sick and tired of feeling stuck, all these emotions gained control of my daily life and I spiraled into a deep depression.

Still grieving for my son Jayden, grieving for my physical loss and coming to the realization this was my normal life now and I needed to adjust. It was too much to bare, that afternoon the family was prepared to go on a short outing, I convinced them I needed some rest, so they can leave me home alone. They all gathered into the car and assured me they will not be away long, if I needed anything to call my neighbor across the street. As I sat on the bed many thoughts went through my head, I waited for the safety call. I knew there would be one phone call that would come through to check on me, after I assured them I was ok I said I love them all and will see them soon.

Little did they know I meant that in the form of when God decided to call them home I would see them soon. As I ended the call I gathered all the medication prescribed to me by the doctor, I poured a handful of them on the bed. Tears began to fill my eyes, I knew that to me life seemed to have dealt me a raw deal and I wanted out. I didn't have the strength to fight anymore, the strength to face another disappointment. I had already lost everything in my eyes, all my emotions have flat lined and I am hopeless. The pain in my body, my mind and my heart took over me, I felt alone no one could understand what I was going through I was better off dead.

As I began to swallow some of the pills I can feel a slight intoxication state creeping up on me, just as I opened my mouth to swallow the second batch of pills my phone rung. The call startled me causing me to drop some of the pills, I never answered the call, but it kept ringing and ringing. Finally, I looked to see who was calling so urgently, surprisingly it was my mother she said I felt in my spirit you needed my help. She had no idea what was taking place on the other end of that call, if the call would have been placed minutes later there would have been no answer.

When I was at my weakest moment and needed help the most, God sent my mother to help me. At times, we struggle to ask for help, but we know that would deny others the blessing of giving. God wired our hearts to give and receive, he gave the ultimate gift he gave sacrificially. He gave from his heart, just as he wants us to give sacrificially and have the grace and humility to receive.

Even though the inner wounds lingered that led me to believe suicide was the only answer. I gathered up enough strength and faith to fight and not allow my circumstances to rob me of my future. It no longer mattered I was in a wheelchair, my hair was gone and I was bald, so what I could not articulate my words correctly, the most important thing was God had a purpose for my life.

I began to work harder at physical therapy, pushing myself beyond my limits. I knew what those doctor's reports said but I was hell bent on proving them wrong, just as they had no hope I would survive, and I still have breath in my body. I have the same chance for a full recovery despite the medical records, the enemy wanted me to be distracted by something God had already finished. Seasons don't last forever and the season I was enduring had nothing to do with my surface.

The harder I worked the more progress I saw, I did so much research on my condition I began doing extra work at night to see more results. My recovery reached 50%, I knew if hard work and determination took me to 50% all I had to do is work two times harder and push myself more and I could reach 100% recovery.

I had reached a point where I wanted to remove anything in my life that would hinder me from being released from the prison of the wheelchair. I contacted the medical equipment company and asked for a walker to be delivered to my home, and any other walking assistant equipment available. As I prepared for my next therapy appointment fear began to creep in, I immediately shut it down with positive self-affirmations.

Reminding myself I can, and I will overcome this tragedy, and I will make it out on top. Through hard work, several weekly therapy sessions and determination, I went from a wheelchair to a walker to a cane and now will walk circles around you with my six-inch heels.

Because of this accident one of the lessons learned was to ask for help when I need it, and when I did God taught me the blessing of receiving. Even though this was the most difficult thing I have ever endured, I'm grateful for the accident, through it I was able to experience heaven, see miracles only God could create, gain a relationship with God and most importantly he spared my life for his purpose.

CHAPTER 6: NEW BEGINNING

Every storm has an end, but in life every end is a new beginning. The joy of the lord is beautiful, I want joy why can't I have joy and trust like David did in the bible? There was something I was always searching for I needed other people to fill a void I felt, men became a piece of meat to me, someone I can conquer. I will become friends with them, use them for my purpose and right when they think they had me I would sting them just like a scorpion.

No one else will break my heart, no one else will abuse me, I am now in control of my own destiny. Then I began to feel a tug, I tried to ignore it, but it just became more intense, God was putting something in my heart, but it was a fight between flesh and my spirit I was refusing.

I began going to church every Sunday, I was still searching for wholeness, I could feel something was missing and a change needed to happen. Honestly it was quite confusing, because I felt like I was losing control of my own life. I remember one time in a quiet place I bowed down to God and asked for forgiveness, I realized I needed to humble myself before him. Going to church on Sunday was not enough, I needed to pray daily surrender my life to God.

I realized prayer and fasting needed to become a necessity not another task, to purify my mind, body and soul to hear from God and change my mentality and view of life, the void in my life could not be filled by a man. That's why I was so frustrated and still searching, the men just were a momentary fix, allowing God's will over my life to be done instead of my own was the only way for me to be complete.

The trials and tribulations of life stole my joy, caused me to be bitter. I cared more about my own happiness than anyone else's, get in my way of what I perceived the will over my life was and you would feel my wrath. The love of God changed all of this for me, if you would have told me seven years ago I would be living for God I would have laughed.

To me living for God meant I could no longer turn up, I had to give up my men toys in my playground. These were men that needed to pay for all my hurt and pain of the past, they would never know what it was like to be intimate with me or have me as their girl because I never allowed them to get that close. Living for God also meant I could no longer treat men like they have treated me in the past, I would have to show compassion to those that broke my heart into pieces.

I wanted no parts of this because then I will have to admit I was broken and would it would require me to release control over my life to someone I can't even see but only hear. I began to idolize success, I needed to be the best at everything I did because never again will there be another failure under my belt. I was invited to a business presentation to speak about my business of health and wellness, there was several different types of businesses represented and everyone gave their sales pitch to convince you to buy their program or product.

Afterwards, I stuck around to introduce myself to everyone and network, that is when I met my sister Yvonne. I know you are wondering why I call her my sister and we met that night, see blood could not make us closer. She is my ram in the bush, Yvonne had no idea when we met what God had in store for her. She needed to save me but that was not any easy task, first I needed to be convinced I needed to be saved.

My birthday was right around the corner and like every year prior I was planning a big event. I rented the biggest VIP section at the club, the one right in front directly on the dance floor separate from the other VIP sections, so when the club was packed everyone could see me and my girls, I was a queen and everything I did was with excellence.

I supplied the space, the food and one top shelf bottle of liquor once that was consumed everyone will chip in to purchase liquor. It was my birthday right so for once let's turn up on someone else's pockets besides mine. Prior to inviting Yvonne, I had no idea she was a double PK (Preacher's Kid), both of her parents are Pastors.

To be honest her whole family are pastors, apostles and ministers, so when she arrived at the club and it seemed like she was in a foreign country. I had to ask are you uncomfortable? She just didn't understand the concept of the night club, so you just come here to dance, get sweaty, drink alcohol, get drunk and go home she asked?

At that point I decided to sit in the comfortable VIP seats and keep Yvonne company, that night was completely different from any night I have ever had at the club. As we sat in VIP and everyone else around us threw back drink after drink and were basically dry humping on the dance floor, me and Yvonne discussed about life, my business, and my family. She shared with me, I had a serious purpose to fulfill and I needed to begin writing.

She handed me a gift bag with a voice recorder inside and said this is for your book, while everyone else wanted to turn up and get drunk Yvonne wanted me to know God had a purpose for my life. It did not matter if we were in a nightclub surrounded by half naked women, drunk men trying to take you home, and everything else you can think of. God had a sense of humor though because he sent me somebody who was so opposite of me.

I'm the queen of etiquette, and my sister is far from it let me tell you, she will fart whenever or wherever she does not care who is around. Her motto is better out than in, I was appalled the first time she did it and we were in public, but she has a heart of gold and will show you the love of Jesus Christ all day, every day.

God sent her into my life for a special task and she was the only person who could handle it. It was time for a new beginning, not just any fresh start but a chance to hope again, God placed a woman in my life who would not be afraid to correct me. If there was something in my life that would keep me from my destiny she would call me on it out of love.

Instead of encouraging my acting out behavior, she was bold enough to smack me in the face with the word and remind me who I was and who I truly represent. So instead of conforming to this world, I would walk in the purpose God has for my life. Yvonne came into my life and immediately saw past all the barriers and knew I needed to tear down the house, I had built.

Life as I knew it would change, it was time to start over knock down what I thought was good for me. I had to tear away the many layers of hurt, regret, pain, and build a house that can withstand any storm. A house built on a solid foundation underneath, my new beginning started with my sister covering me, going into her pray closet on my behalf. She saw greatness on my life, not just going out having a good time, going on trips but changing people's lives.

Sharing my testimony with other women, telling them how they can overcome any trial and tribulation in their life. I began attending different churches, I wanted to find a place I belong and not just attend a church because it's familiar to someone else who lead me there. There is not one religion I did not visit outside of Christianity, I studied the Mormon faith, Jehovah Witness, Buddha, Muslim, and the list goes on. Life had beat me up and I was on a mission to find what was missing out of my life.

During my journey I learned self-love, gained a positive mindset about myself, and my life regardless of my past, and my journey which once was taking me on the wrong path was transformed. I had lost myself over the years, in motherhood, relationships, hardships and loss, I began to attend conferences to build me up as a woman. Help me continue to improve my mindset regarding love, marriage and men.

Even though I had failed, I began to hope again that I would be a wife again and have a successful marriage, but I needed guidance and knowledge. When I reached a point where I had a successful career, I had a high level of self-love, I came to grips with my past and made peace with it. I even began to prepare myself and my surroundings for my future, I had reached a point where I reconnected with my dreams and I began to dream bigger than I could ever believe was possible.

I began to get uncomfortable, try new things and meet new people. I developed a daily prayer life and reading the word, I just became hungry for more of God, I was tired of everything old I had found my happy place. My life around me began to look different, I was surrounded by signs and messages that will inspire me. I realized I had the power to be, or have and do anything I desired.

There are people in this world that are sent to help you move from the place of brokenness and walk in purpose. God sent my sister Yvonne to be my ram in the bush, God did not save my life for my testimony to be washed away by getting drunk, have a bad attitude and living by the society standards. Change was upon me; a warrior was sent to me by my heavenly father to help fight for me in the war of life because I was not strong enough to see the war or fight alone.

All I wanted to do is survive, I became comfortable where I was at that I was stuck and not progressing. I know it looked like I was doing well, I drove a Range Rover, had thousands in my accounts, traveled all around the world when I felt like it, weekly shopping sprees, but it was not living at the level God intended for my life.

When my life began to transform, I knew it had nothing to do with me and God was showing out in my life. There were gifts inside of me that needed to be birthed out of me, all I had to is give God total control over my life. Starting fresh is a bit scary, it makes me apprehensive because the future is unknown. I wonder if I am up for the task, if I will catch another disappointment to discourage me and derail my progress, but I know as I embrace a new beginning I will grow and change to become the women God gave life to a second time and live out his will over my life.

I have a uniquely designed purpose in life, and so do you.

CHAPTER 7: MY # 7 DIVINE COMPLETION AND PERFECTION

Number seven is used 735 times in the bible, 54 times in the book of revelation alone. The number seven is the foundation of God's word, seven is the number of completeness and perfection both physically and spiritually. Most of my life I needed a man and earthly possessions to complete me and make me feel worthy, if I had the best car, plenty of money, the designer labels in clothing, and so on that made me feel like I meant something.

As if these things said you have made it, the more my personal relationship with God grew the more I realized no one or nothing can validate me but God. I had reached a point where I threw myself into being successful within my career, there was no point in dating relationships didn't work.

I have lived through two serious relationships that I thought were forever and I gave all the love I could give, but they still failed. Then in-between those relationships I had four hook up buddies, we shall call them. You know the ones you are not in a relationship with, but if you have an event you need to attend you hit them up or there is a new movie coming out and you want company to watch it.

These were not a Netflix and chill type of relationship, just call a friend when you need one, yea that type (laughing). There was no potential for life partner in any of those gentlemen either, so when I set my mind that slot seven would be forever closed and I would remain single because there was no perfect match to complete me. The void I was looking to fill could only be satisfied by a relationship with my heavenly father. God was my number seven, he completed me not men.

I began to spend time with God and learn for myself who he was, it's funny how over time when you realize who you are, your language, posture, and mindset changes. You begin to realize you are royalty and you must act and think within those standards. I realized God was the one I was searching for, the only one who could fill the emptiness that caused my spirit unrest. He is the one perfect piece of a puzzle that I never could seem to find, that one guy I yearned to hold onto and was all mine, one that would never leave me and love me.

All the searching I did for nothing, when all I needed was to be still, God's love that overcame me felt like that one perfect song that makes my heart skip a beat and speaks to my soul. It takes me deeper within myself to a point where I see the beauty of living, you complete me and not man or material possessions.

God showed me he is everything I ever dreamed and hoped for, he knew my weaknesses and covered them, he knew the good, the bad and the ugly of my past and present, he looked past it all and saw his beautiful creation. He knows my happy and dark thoughts, but he loves me regardless of my imperfections and does not judge me.

He is my number seven, a match made in heaven. His love humbled me, he began to speak sweet words to me during my silence to encourage my weary spirit. His faith in me gave me hope, God saw me at my worst, yet he is focused on the good he knows what I carry within me. He sees in me what I could not previously see in myself.

When I rest in his presence, I see beauty and experience a peace I could never explain. At that moment I am aware how safely you hold my heart, you are everything I ever needed, and I shall want no more. It's the first time, I completely let go of my guards closed my eyes and had an unexplainable experience. God is and will always be the only thing I need to complete me, I was no longer afraid of love, marriage, life, failure, or anything else that would come in my path.

God had placed his hands over my life, he was so good to me. I had no idea what my future held but I knew I could not do it without him. I can do all things through Christ which strengthened me. (Philippians 4:13)

CHAPTER 8: I BELIEVE IN MIRACLES

When God steps in miracles happen.

For a long time, there was so much turmoil in my life. It saddens me to think of the years and energy I wasted searching for what I already had in God. Thankfully I came to a place where I loved myself, even though life hasn't been easy. Despite it all, I managed to keep my head up and continue fighting throughout I was proud of everything, I went through and mostly who I have become.

Even though the process was not easy it was necessary to become the women God intended for me to be. I needed to suffer for a while for God to perfect me, I once was lost but I am now found. I survived the attack and now it is time to receive my blessings, it was a purpose behind all my pain. I found myself starting to live out my dreams, I became a business owner of a Nutrition

Club where people would gather to have a healthy nutritional meal replacement shake to reach their goals.

I created an oasis where people can enter the doors, and suddenly they would forget all about the bad day they had. The argument with their spouse, the kids acting up and all the other life challenges they endured that day. The nutrition club was not just me helping others, but it also allowed me to help broken people enter through my doors and find hope, motivation and a positive atmosphere. I met some amazing people who owned businesses next to me, behind me and in front of me. We all were like a community, supporting each other businesses, referring our clients to patron our neighbors. Some owners even played the dating game from time to time, when they thought a match made in heaven was possible.

Located three doors down from my storefront was a barbershop that was owned by master barber Smittee, we became good friends and we both would patronage each other businesses, this allowed us to grow our new customer goals each month. I can remember one day at work, I was preparing with my business partner to go do a presentation. As we walked down the hallway, we passed my friends barbershop I heard the gentleman in the chair ask who is that? My friend which is his barber said which one the Latin lady, and he replies no the chocolate one.

We left to go do our presentation, upon returning Smittee came and brought me a business card belonging to her client. At first, I refused to accept the card, I was not looking or in the market for a new relationship or any new friends for that matter. My mindset was focused on growing my business, being a mother, and a date was not only a distraction but the furthest thing from my mind. Smittee, "The Master Barber" as she likes to be called, insisted that I call her client, she explained how he was such a great guy and was wondering how she missed the opportunity to connect us. Eventually I gave in and I called him, our initial conversation went so well it was like we met before.

After spending over eight hours talking about life, our future goals, and our past we realized for the last six years we have lived in the same area more than twice and his family knew my family. We had lots of similarities and testimonies, our conversations and time spent was like a breath of fresh air. Even though I was not interested in a relationship, whatever this was seemed different, but I was wise enough not to jump in and be blindsided again.

I decided to do something different with this situation, in case it turned into a relationship. Something I have never done before, you know what they say doing the same thing over and over expecting a different result is insanity right? Well insanity no longer resided in my life, so I went to God for guidance. Making that decision changed my vision for this courtship, I began to see things about Esteban I could not see before with my natural eye.

The more time we spent together, the more God revealed to me. God showed me he would be my protector, Esteban was given the gift of sight. He had the ability to see into the spirit realm and view people for who they truly were. He began to warn me about certain people I had around me, that would not be able to go with me to the next level. We both had a relationship with God, but it was not where it should be, at that time neither of us knew about the Holy Spirit, demonic attacks, spiritual warfare, these things were foreign to us both. We both were raised in the Catholic church, so the more he would tell me I would get angry like he was trying to keep me from my friends.

The enemy knew what was inside of Esteban and who he was, so I would always hear a voice telling me he is just like the rest of them trying to change you. Let him go he will mess your life up, different things all the time would come to me and I would pray and ask for clarity. God would show me something totally different about Esteban then I would clearly hear a voice telling me to run, the more I prayed to God ask is this the man you want in my life? The more he would reveal Esteban's heart to me, we were one year into our relationship and decided to drive my mother to Atlanta for a weekend visit with her brother Kenneth.

We all spent the weekend laughing, shopping, and spending time together. That Saturday night we all went out to dinner; my uncle Ken chose Pappadeaux seafood kitchen. This placed was packed, there was a fifty-five-minute wait for seating, my uncle Ken asked if we wanted to wait it would be worth it. I had no idea what this night had in store for me. The restaurant was packed almost to capacity, we finally were seated after such a long wait.

By the time the waiter arrived at our table, we were starving and quickly placed our drink and food order. As we all patiently waited on our food, we talked about my uncle recent tour with the Army oversees, discussing his experience made me appreciate everything the men and women of our United States military do daily.

During our conversation my uncle phone beeped, and he began to smile, as Esteban raised up out of his seat to go to the restroom, so I thought. As he turned away, he stepped back and grabbed my hand, my stomach dropped you know that feeling when you are on a roller coaster and it sends you plunging down a deep drop at 100 MPH, that feeling was all over me.

I immediately covered my face, I believe I knew what was about to happen, but I didn't want to jump to conclusions. Esteban asked me to stand as he held my hand, as I looked around there were over 100 people watching and waiting along with me to see what was going on. When I stood up Esteban had both of my hands in his hands and began to profess his love for me. The water works began as he went down on one knee in front of my family and a restaurant filled of people all looking with anticipation.

I was captured by the moment, even though I was married before I have never been proposed to. I didn't know what it felt like to have someone profess their love for you in front of a room full of strangers, I knew what words were supposed to follow when he was on one knee, but I could not hear him speaking. I was only able to look into his eyes and God showed me my husband, my future, as I opened my mouth I screamed Yes Yes Yes!

That weekend would change my life and the dynamics of my family. We returned home on cloud nine after such a great weekend, an engagement meant it was time to get down to business, we spoke intensely before about our goals and desires for our family and future.

The wedding planning was a fun process all the way to the alter. I remember one night being in Target looking at towels for our new life together, and I found Esteban in the baby section picking out a girl's onesie. I was a little confused because we had the conversation that I could not bear any more children, he began to tell me how God showed him our family and we had another child and it was a girl.

He brought the onesie, and placed it in his closet to stand on God's promise. Shortly after the wedding I found out I was pregnant, we had a honeymoon baby just as we planned. Just as my husband said God showed him we were having a girl, life was amazing. I had finally found my Boaz and he truly loved me as Christ loved the church.

When things seem to be perfect, there is always a storm waiting to happen. The more I molded into my new life and growing as a new wife, the more situations would begin to pull me and my husband apart. Prior to this marriage I was the head of household, with my children and other family members who lived in my home. My family was always there, I could not imagine life without them. Family get togethers were plentiful but there always seemed to be an elephant in the room.

When my husband was around there was always little chatter, I could not figure it out. They adore the man that could have killed me and still ask how he is doing, then we have the husband that could not keep his vows because he needed a variety of women, they bake him cakes and pies and always invite him to function's. Then we have the current husband who would give his life for mine, treats me like a wife that's the one you dislike. I was confused but mostly hurt and I would get emotional over this situation, what was I supposed to do?

When I looked for help by people I trust, I was reminded of the scripture Genesis 2:25 "Therefore, a man shall leave his father and his mother and hold fast to his wife, and they shall become one flesh." I had some amazing God lead married couples in my life speaking life into me and my husband. We were newlyweds and all hell had broken loose in our marriage.

My adult son showed my husband no respect and put him down every chance he got. He went so far as to try and convince his younger sister who was still living at home to be disrespectful as well. My family members openly began to discuss their disapproval of my husband which was disrespectful to my marriage. My cousin would call me and keep me informed of the conversations that were spoken, and let me know no one like him, I was truly surprised at two of the women in my family that made comments. They were the reason I existed, it certainly changed our relationships, especially since they didn't know my husband and never spent time with him but made judgements.

It had got to a point where I began to turn on my husband as well, I felt like my family was being ripped away from me because of my husband. I began to feel resentment towards my husband and marriage. This toxic behavior went on for an extended period, it had broken our peaceful bond, we allowed the enemy to come right in and destroy what God had put together.

I felt like I was bonded to my family and what made this so different? I was married before and remained in relationship with my blood relatives, I had to learn when you are bonded to certain things you lose some of your spiritual discernment. You begin to be in spiritual blindness, and that's how the enemy prevails over you.

I was allowing myself to be moved emotionally every time my husband would speak the truth about what was going on, it's because I was in bondage. I needed to be matured so I would not be moved emotionally but see what was really going on, the enemy wanted me to stay in darkness allowing my family disapproval and chitter chatter to wedge me and my husband apart. Keeping me in the dark he can guide me in the direction he wants me to go, so we as one would not reach our spiritual position.

I quickly forgot that the day I became Mrs. Rushing I was unified with Esteban and we became one flesh. We were now one in purpose, one in mind, and one in unity. As I was taught by my sister Yvonne and my spiritual mother Apostle Moton what it meant to be a wife, I had a hard pill to swallow. I realized that I had allowed the thoughts of others to drive me to tear down my husband, if we are one flesh then I was also tearing myself down.

I realized I was wrong and I needed to do damage control, I had hurt the one person who loved me because during the first two years of my marriage I was playing devil's advocate, trying to keep my family happy and my husband. I wanted everyone happy, if someone was disrespectful to my husband he would just have to defend himself. Nobody came before blood, so I thought, when you know better you do better.

The more I stayed under the leadership of my spiritual mother the more my eyes were opened. I need to first ask God for forgiveness, then seek it from my husband. As I began to build him back up, I saw the joy return this was not an easy process because I completely pulled away from my family. The minute I realized who I was as a wife, my mindset changed first, then everything around me fell in place.

I began to hear talk about how Esteban changed

me, I saw Facebook posts about me and all because no one understood that it was not my husband that changed me. The word of God changed me, that is my husband and finally someone sat me down and taught me what it meant to be a wife.

I can remember being at my aunt Yvonne's house and she shared with me she would go off on anyone who disrespected her husband. I was learning scripture and Godly principles, this was unusual to my family, they had never experienced me being submissive to my husband, my life being in alignment God first, my husband, then my children in that order.

I was ridiculed and talked about for protecting what God put together. I noticed my entire life was flipped upside down when I began to live as one flesh, doors began to open and the ones that needed to be closed were shut. Me and my husband saw that apart our foundation would crumble but if we stood strong together we were a force to be reckoned with.

Our prayer time with God increased together and separately, we knew we could not let our guards down. Our purpose together was so great that the enemy used what was close to me to try and destroy our union. He almost had me, but my sister Yvonne was on her post as a gatekeeper, and told me she doesn't care who comes against my husband don't allow them to disrespect him.

When I began to pray for my husband and pray that the issue with my family would cease, I saw how the more I prayed for Esteban and became unbothered about family issues. God elevated us to the next level, I look back and realize if I had the wrong people around me I would be divorced. It's imperative you surround yourself with goal orientated, like-minded people.

I have learned you must meditate on the word of god, read the word and see how it will change the world around you but also how it will transform your life.

Just like me you will wake up one day amazed at the current life you live because you know what it used to look like. I was bold enough to stand against people I love wholeheartedly, and stand on the word of God and live my life as a wife submissive to her husband as he is submissive to God. When I lived out the word of God it was a shift in my life and my house, everything around me that was not of God had to flee. Everyone who was not in line with the path me and my husband was on was removed, the more I prayed the more people around us talked about the ultimate change. Even some of my family saw our Christ like foundation we built and asked God and us to forgive them for anything said against us.

Martha Rushing

You must know the power of your prayers as a kingdom citizen, something wonderful and marvelous is going to happen in your life, when you develop a relationship with God and stand on His Word.

CHAPTER 9: TOTAL SURRENDER

Let go and let God work. You get to a point in your life where you want change, I went through everything you can think of and it was time for me to just allow God to guide me. Up until this point, I don't think I did a fantastic job on my own.

One morning during my reading time I heard consecration, I had no idea what that was. Google is your best friend when you need to know anything, so I looked it up. Even though it was a little confusing I called my spiritual mom Apostle Moton and explained to her I believe God is telling me to go into a consecration, she began to weep because little did I know she was praying I would go after God deeper than I was.

We prayed, and God gave us the exact direction of what he wanted me to do. I remember trying to negotiate with the instructions, I needed to log off Facebook, Email, and all other social media sites. My instructions were meant to push me into an uncomfortable place. I had to seclude myself from the outside world, this meant walking away from my business, which is my only source of income.

I was terrified, God wanted me to give up everything that was familiar to me. I was in the process of a pay raise in my business, I had an entire team that depended on me. I cried out to God because I felt like he was stripping everything I worked so hard for away from me, I felt like I was letting people in my life down.

I had never fully given anyone in my life control over me, but this was a requirement from God. After I was done having a pity party I was obedient, I went to the nutrition club which was the place I conducted my business and packed up all my stuff quietly. I did not make a big scene, I placed everything in my vehicle and tried to leave quickly so no one would question me.

Later that day the questions did come as expected, just like I assumed I was letting people down and losing friends that were like family to me. I did not understand God's purpose.

If I'm totally honest, I will even say I began to get a little angry just when I was at a point where I was allowing God to move. I could clearly hear the voice of the enemy saying to me if he loves you then why is he taking everything away. You should go back to your business, if you don't your family will struggle.

I had enough sense to go in my prayer closet, I had spent enough time with my father to know his voice over every other voice. I was honest with God and talk to him like he was my home-girl, God what did I do wrong that everything I loved has been stripped away? His answer was very clear because I put them before him, I was told to look at every social media site I operated and find a post where I was praising him for my testimony and leading souls to his kingdom.

I had become so focused on succeeding, I was not sharing with anyone where God brought me from. I immediately prayed and asked for forgiveness then began to thank God for loving me enough to strip me from everything and bring me into submission for his will over my life to be done. During my time in heaven while in a coma, I was told there were people waiting to hear my story.

Heavenly Father gave me life again to help others have everlasting life through Jesus Christ and I was more focused on my financial growth instead of my kingdom assignment and winning souls for Christ. At this point I knew that for me to totally surrender God had to help me because my flesh wanted to be rebellious.

I needed to remove all my thoughts and desires so God could fill me up, I realized that Martha had to die. All my life I have been traveling down roads that lead me to hurt, disappointment, abuse, suicide, and death so taking my hands off the wheel was that such a bad thing. Looking at my track record, I was not doing a great job or living up to my full potential.

Once I died to myself, I asked God to change the mind of all the people around me. Make the people around me start to think I'm lame now, and all I want to do now is go to church and read my bible. I began to ask God to be my protector against the people that would block me because if they can't connect to where I'm going then we cannot be in a relationship with each other.

God has a plan for my life and everyone is not ready or equipped to be Bonnie and Clyde with me on this journey, I'm in this season with God where I'm seeking and trusting him for everything and I can't handle any distractions to throw me off course. As I am trusting God, everything I thought he stripped from me he gave back to me through my husband.

When I did exactly what God wanted me to do, my husband received a raise that is unheard of. Even his manager was surprised, but it came out to the same amount monthly that I was making from my business. The more I went after God the more me and my husband connected on a level we never connected before, God began to bring broken people to us that needed to hear our testimony, so they can hold on to the word of God and know that the same God that created miracles in our lives will be the same God that will turn their lives around.

Sometimes we need others to lead us to the word of God when we are going through we have to remember the enemy believes everything that is written in our bible and knows the truth of the word. What a shame it would be for the enemy to believe more in our potential than we do ourselves.

We all face battles but when you realize the greatness that is on your life, it's hard to allow your head to hang low the true lesson is when you realize how fearful the enemy is of you because of your greatness. Your battle seems so minor and that sack of bricks seems to go away.

I have fought many battles in my life, searched high and low trying to find my worth and figure out who I am and what purpose I served on this earth. Then I realized everything I needed was inside my life manual the bible, I realized I already had victory over every situation. Embedded in these two verses Exodus 14:13-14 There is promise for victory, God does not say you have to fight for it or figure out how to gain victory.

All you must do is follow the simple steps to claim the victory that God has already claimed for you. I constantly found myself dealing with trials and tribulations, even though it took years I realized it was time for change.

Often there are emotions, people, even situations we are attached to that need to be removed. Until these things are removed we will remain in bondage. God wanted to take me to a new level, but I needed to be transformed from an immature state of mind to a phenomenal woman of God. Going through a metamorphosis process becoming a person unknown to everyone familiar to me but walking in excellence according to God's will.

During my process of growing pains, and allowing myself to die to the woman I once was to become the women I was destined to be I suffered a great deal, experienced sorrow, and loneliness. The only way I could have victory through the process was by feeding myself with the word every day and night. I had to completely humble myself as I completely surrender to God.

Prior to me taking my hands off my life, I was comfortable in doing the same thing over and over without getting a different result. I was so comfortable that God could not elevate me to the next level, I was so busy concentrating on everything around me, my business, my family issues, my children, and making sure others saw my value.

I didn't know that God wanted all of me, I was ok with giving him parts of me hoping he would treasure what I offered. The moment I gave God the same love, I wanted to receive everything changed. I loved him, worshipped him, regardless if I had $10,000 in my account or $10. Through sickness and health, Good times and bad times.

The same love and attention I gave he returned it ten times over, he needed to renew my mind, body and soul so his greatness can be heard through my testimony.

I surrendered and once again God gave me life only this time I was not physically dying but spiritually dying and he saved me.

CHAPTER 10: GRACE GOD

God treated me like I have never sinned. As I prepare for the world to read my truth, I reflect on all the life lessons I have had in my life 37 years of life. I worked very hard not to become a statistic society has about teenage mothers, I tried very hard all throughout my life for people to see my value and look past all my mistakes.

I often ask myself why did I have the desire to fit in so badly? What value did I see in others that I needed their validation, they were trying to figure life out just like me.

I had so many insecurities, I would make fun of myself put myself down and call myself names. If others said something that was demeaning, I would join in on the jokes self-inflicting more pain. I trained myself with words to feel less than who I really was, there is much power in the words we speak over ourselves.

I had so many wounds that were not healed I would attract other insecure people. We would try to make one whole person out of the broken pieces, the more I tried the worse my life became, I stayed in both of my broken relationships because I believed that's what I deserved. Then I would tell myself you have to stay for the children, you did not grow up without a father in your home don't subject your children to a broken home.

I would suck up any sorrows I had and just endure, I was broken, tired, frustrated, and insecure but I was also a mother. I was used to putting everyone before myself, so life was bearable if I convinced myself leaving would devastate the children. I was bleeding and heartbroken but willing to continue for my children happiness.

Then I realized, I underestimated my children. My unhappiness was not so hidden, and it began to show in their school work, my unspoken secrets were not as secret as I thought. I had a decision to make either stay in misery or live in peace by leaving. With each failed relationship, I felt like a failure to my mate and children. I so badly wanted to be a good wife and mother, but I was not being successful at either, I can honestly say I did not leave because of abuse, betrayal, or cheating but because I wanted to be loved.

You know that love that you run home to the kind of love that has butterflies in your belly. One day I realized that the love I could give is not the same love returned to me, it was a counterfeit version and I could not settle my entire life.

When I was transitioning into my new lifestyle as a single mom, I wanted to help other young women like myself avoid my mistakes and the road I traveled, by sharing my journey with them. I didn't realize I would begin to heal as well, I think speaking with the young women of Precious Gems allowed me to see myself in them.

When I would listen to their stories, I would think what would I tell the younger me if I had a chance to speak with her and avoid the hardship. Precious Gems gathered every third Saturday of each month, the more I worked with the young ladies the more I gained back more of my self-confidence.

All my life I avoided letting people know my ugly truth, I hid very well being the representative I created for the world to see. Funny how life turns you around sometimes, the very thing I avoided was the same thing that saved me in the end.

Every chance I shared my truth I became whole, I realized God put these young women in my life for a purpose. My healing purpose had begun without my knowledge, but when you find God you will find peace, health, food, riches, everything you need in life.

God should have the first place in our lives, we need to seek him and desire him not just for what he can do for us but to worship and love him.

On paper my life is far from perfect, it is a hot mess. In my search for the perfect fairy tale ending I lost myself, took a detour off the road God had for me and I went missing from reality. Even though I thought I was too far gone God found me and showed me grace.

I didn't think, I deserved his grace me the teen mother, divorcee, reckless behavior, attempted suicide. I was stuck in who I once was not knowing I could survive my past and God could mend my broken heart. His grace sustained me past who I was and allowed me to collide with my destiny.

God's grace allowed me to fall in love with him, fall in love with myself and when I look at me I could see myself as God saw me. I no longer saw my mistakes and I stopped making my journey about myself, God was using me the little bit I offered he took and began to show me purpose and destiny.

I was overwhelmed with the grace of God and gave him all my fears, insecurities, my past and my life. I gave up the idea that I needed to be this perfect person for God, during my need to be perfect I realized all he ever wanted was me.

Everything I went through was not in vain, God was doing something on the inside. The pain is worth it, the struggle is worth it, the loss is worth it, God knew he could trust me with the testimony and in the end, he would get all the glory.

Sometimes when I reflect on my journey I remember the story of Ruth in the bible she had to keep moving forward trusting her lord and savior who she barely knew. She lost everything but instead of becoming bitter, stuck or content she gathered herself together and moved forward.

No one would fault me if I was still lost, I mean I have been beaten, cheated on, lost my son and nearly died. An average person would have lost their mind, at one point I did forget who I was and lost every bit of faith but I had to realize something important.

We cannot allow our past, our mistakes, our sin or our fear to keep us from going after the things of God.

God can turn your life around in your favor. If he did all this for me imagine what he has in store for you, make the decision today to surrender your all to God.

Past, present, future and watch how your life changes when you begin to build a relationship with your heavenly father. I'm not sure what God has in store for me, the difference now is I'm not afraid. I'm ready to encounter any journey he has set for me, because I know I can do all things through Christ who strengthens me as it states in Philippians 4:13.

If God can strengthen me, restore me, and heal me to collide with my destiny he can and will do the same for you.

Like a caterpillar you will be transformed into a beautiful butterfly, trust the process.

CONCLUSION

My prayers are that this book gave you hope, built your faith stronger, and through my journey you had an eye-opening experience for your own life. I know we all have our own stories of overcoming, through it all we must push forward. There are others behind us depending on our success, so they know they can succeed as well.

Your mind may tell you it's impossible, or who do you think you are it's never going to happen for you. Deep down inside you have this burning sensation stirring up, it wakes you up at night and leaves you restless.

That's the promise of God calling you, it's time for you to collide with your destiny, God loves you too much to allow you to settle or live an average life. He will push you into your greatness, and you will give birth to the treasure hidden inside of you.

Imagine letting go of all frustration, anger, resentment and worry, giving it all to God, imagine the freedom you will feel. Imagine having no bitterness or envy, no anxiety and no fear.

Imagine the immense positive power of not being held back by negativity, that is all possible and it is possible right now with God. You have imagined it and you can just as surely live it.

Of course, all sorts of disappointing, frustrating, and discouraging things happen in life on a daily basis. Yet there is no good reason to hold on to the negativity in your life.

You must grow to become successful in any part of your life, that means you must be willing to do what most people won't. They are unwilling to be pushed beyond their comfort zone, I won't mislead you into thinking this is an easy process.

When you are stretched it hurts but the rewards are great, the only thing standing in your way is you. Release the champion inside and soar like an eagle.

About The Author

Broke But Not Broken

Martha is a native of New York prior to her family relocating to North Carolina, she is the Founder and Chief Operational Officer of Healing Hearts Inc and Butterfly Nation Ministries. She represents several universities across North Carolina, but her educational background, dean list certificates, psychology courses could not prepare her for life's twist and turns. Life experiences have molded her into the women she is today and she has a natural gift that cannot be taught or purchased in any store. Her passion for making a difference in the lives of men, women and children in her community who are in need has been evident over the years through her community work. However, her true passion is inspiring others to reach for their unlimited potential. As a motivational speaker, she has delivered hundreds of empowering messages to thousands of individuals in schools, organizations, conferences, and faith based institutions.

Martha is a wife, mother, and life coach, During the last ten years she has spent most of her free time advocating for rape and domestic violence victims, she has also spent countless hours teaching young girls in her community about image, personal hygiene, being responsible and respectful, and to always carry themselves as ladies.

Her vision is to empower, nurture and inspire others through whatever transition of life they currently are in. Martha has dedicated and devoted her time to others in her community assisting them with their personal, emotional and social needs, in addition she holds workshops, conferences, community events, and group sessions to individuals within her organization.

Martha Rushing is a member of New Beginnings Ministries in Charlotte, NC. The National Association of Professional woman, and also a member of The Association of Professional Leaders of Women and Girls. Martha has been a Life Coach for over nine years helping others reach their full potential, while becoming better versions of themselves.

Martha Rushing

Martha is committed to making a difference in her community, after a tragic event in her life she decided to use the second chance God gave her at life and what she endured as an inspirational tool to teach others no matter what cards you're dealt in life, your future depends on your desire, motivation, and dedication to reach beyond your grasp.

She believes both tears and sweat are salty, but they render a different result. Tears will get you sympathy; Sweat will get you change. For things to change, you must first change your mindset, she does not know the key to success, but believes the key to failure is falling and not getting back up.

You can follow Martha at Butterfly Nation on Facebook or email her at martha.healinghearts@gmail.com

Broke But Not Broken

Empowerment Authors Book Store

Empowerment Publishing & Multi-media produces children's books to inspire, uplift and empower our children to greatness. If you have a story that needs to be told that will inspire a child, let us help you to tell it. We offer coaching/publishing packages to suit the beginner and the vet! Our youngest author was only 7 year old! If she can do it, so can you!!

Empowerment Authors Book Store

We also publish stories of overcoming, and empowerment, self-help and personal development. Our unique model provides the author with writing support and structuring a business around their book so that they can make the most impact with their story. You lived through it, now use it to EMPOWER others!!

Contacts us at:
author@ePublishYou.com

The EPMM Speakers Bureau can bring authors to your live or virtual event. For more information or to book an event contact the EPMM Speakers Bureau at 704-493-2035 or via email contact: Producers@ePublishYou.com

67552364R00067

Made in the USA
Columbia, SC
29 July 2019